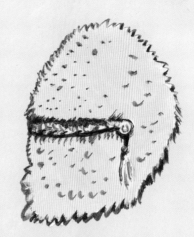

For Bob —J.S.

To Ian and Anna —K.H.

Text copyright © 2017 by Judy Sierra
Jacket art and interior illustrations copyright © 2017 by Kevin Hawkes

Visit us on the Web! randomhousekids.com

Educators and librarians, for a variety of teaching tools, visit us at
RHTeachersLibrarians.com

Library of Congress Cataloging-in-Publication Data
is available upon request.

ISBN 978-0-553-51097-3 (trade) — ISBN 978-0-375-97429-8 (lib. bdg.) —
ISBN 978-0-553-51098-0 (ebook)
MANUFACTURED IN CHINA
10 9 8 7 6 5 4 3 2 1
First Edition

Random House Children's Books supports the First Amendment and
celebrates the right to read.

IMAGINE THAT!

How Dr. Seuss Wrote *The Cat in the Hat*

by Judy Sierra

illustrated by Kevin Hawkes

RANDOM HOUSE 🏠 NEW YORK

1954 was a great year to be a kid.
There were five-cent doughnuts and
one-cent lollipops. Rock and roll had just
hit the record shops. Bookstores brimmed
with exciting new books, like *Charlotte's Web*,
The Lord of the Rings, and *Horton Hears a Who!*

1954 was a great year to be a kid, unless you were trying to learn how to read. For some reason, first graders weren't making the leap from reading a few words to reading a whole book. Grown-ups were stumped. What could the problem be? Kids knew the answer: School readers were just plain boring.

A famous writer named John Hersey agreed with the kids. He had an idea for solving the problem and wrote about it in *Life* magazine.

What kids needed was a beginning reader so exciting that they couldn't stop turning the pages. Who could write a book like that? Only the funniest children's author in the land . . .

Dr. Seuss!

And
Another
Any
Are
As
Asked
At
Away
Back
Bad
Ball
Be
Bed
Bent
Bet
Big
Bit
Bite
Book
Books
Bow
Box
Bump
Bumps
But
Cake
Call
Came
Can
Cat
Cold
Come
Could
Cup

Gone
Good
Got
Gown
Had
Hall
Hand
Hands
Has
Hat
Have
He
Head
Hear
Her
Here
High
Him
His
Hit
Hold
Home
Hook
Hop
Hops
House
How
I
If
In
Into
Is
It
Jump
Jumps

Near
Net
New
No
Not
Nothing
Now
Of
Oh
On
One
Our
Out
Pack
Pat
Pick
Picked
Pink
Play
Playthings
Plop
Pot
Put
Rake
Ran
Red
Rid
Run
Sad
Said

My
Tell
That
The
The
The
The
The
The
Thin
Thin
Think
This
Those
Thump
Thumps
Tip
To
Too
Top
Toy
Trick
Tricks
Two
Up
Us
Wall
Want
Was
Way

Dr. Seuss, we insist!
Won't you please write a book that no kid can resist?
P.S. Use the words on this No-Nonsense List.

Ted, as he was known to his friends, had
already published nine big picture books, books
like *If I Ran the Zoo* and *Scrambled Eggs Super!* and
Thidwick the Big-Hearted Moose. They were funny
and kids loved them.

But could he write and illustrate
a first-grade reader?

Of course! A short little book
like that would only take one or two
weeks . . .

. . . or so he thought.

Each morning after breakfast, Ted went upstairs to his studio. He had a chair and a desk, a drawing board for drawing, and a typewriter for writing.

He also had a closet full of outlandish hats.
When he couldn't think of the right words,
a suitable hat was sure to help.

Writing a beginning reader was not as simple
as it seemed. For one thing, Ted liked to invent
new words for his books, words like

Oobleck and
It-Kutch and
YERKA and Wombus
and Hippo-No-Hungus and
Dippo-No-Dungus.

But in this book, he would only be able
to use words from . . .

THE
OFFICIAL
LIST

"I shall write a rip-roaring book about a queen
zebra," Ted declared. He checked the official list.
Queen? No, not on the list.
Zebra? No, not on the list.
"Maybe a book about a bird. I like birds!"
Bird? Not on the list? No-o-o-o-o!

Ted glared at the list. He spied the word *cat*, and he spied the word *hat*.

"*Cat* rhymes with *hat*, so I'll just start with that!"

He reached for his crayons and his colored pencils.

The cat needed a whiz-bang story. Ted doodled (his stories often began with a doodle). He daydreamed. He tapped at the keys of his typewriter. He donned several hats as he sat in his chair and stared at the list.

In his head, Ted juggled the words on the list.
Then he thought,

Why not let the *cat* juggle instead?
He can juggle the stuff on the list. Yes, he can!
He can juggle a rake and a book and a fan.
He can juggle a fish, and the fish won't like *that*.
I will draw two nice kids to have fun with the cat,
And two naughty Things, and a keen cleaner-upper.
I think I'll get started tonight, after supper.

Ted pondered how kids learned to read. He had a hunch that easy rhymes and funny drawings would help them guess the words they didn't know. He used tricks to coax readers to turn the pages. For example, he put the word *BUMP* in huge letters at the top-right edge of page five. What made that BUMP sound? Kids had to turn the page to find out.

Ted drew. He redrew.
He wrote. He revised. It took
more than a year until he was
satisfied that the book was
funny enough, and exciting
enough, and all-around
stupendous enough for kids
learning to read.

Ted delivered the manuscript to his
publishers in New York. They loved it!
Soon, huge sheets of paper rolled
off giant printing presses. Workers used
special machines to fold the paper, cut it
into pages, sew the pages together, and
sandwich each book between two covers.
They loaded the books onto trucks, and
the trucks rumbled away to libraries,
bookstores, and schools.

It didn't take long for the news to spread from kid to kid, from coast to coast. There was a new book, an easy book, a book that was so much fun, you just couldn't stop reading it. Everyone had to have a copy of *The Cat in the Hat*.

Ted traveled to Boston, New York, and Chicago to meet kids, sign their books, and give autographs. The first-grade reader was a smashing success. He had done it! He had created a fantastic book using only 236 different words.

But the great Dr. Seuss didn't stop there.
No. He wrote a sequel, *The Cat in the Hat
Comes Back*. And he started to publish more
books for kids who were beginning to read.

One day, Ted's friend Bennett Cerf
proposed the ultimate challenge. He bet
that Ted couldn't write a beginning reader
using only fifty different words.

Could he? Would he?

Yes! In fact, he could do it here or there.
He could do it anywhere, with the help of a
clever young fellow named Sam-I-am and a
whopping big serving of green eggs and ham.

Imagine that!

WRITING AND ILLUSTRATING TIPS FROM DR. SEUSS

1. **Set yourself a challenging goal.**

   "All I needed, I figured, was to find a whale of an exciting subject which would make the average six-year-old want to read like crazy."

2. **Draw on your strengths.**

   "The truth is that I like dogs better than cats, but I don't know how to draw a dog."

   (Dr. Seuss was exaggerating, of course, as he often did in interviews. He drew a perfectly wonderful dog for *How the Grinch Stole Christmas!*)

3. **Stir up story ideas by doodling.**

   "Mine always start as a doodle. I may doodle a couple of animals. If they bite each other, it's going to be a good book. If you doodle enough, the characters begin to take over themselves—after a year and a half or so."

4. **Recycle, recycle, recycle.**

5. **Revise, revise, revise.**

   "To produce a 60-page book, I may easily write more than 1,000 pages before I'm satisfied. . . . Write, rewrite, reject, re-reject, and polish incessantly."

A NOTE FROM
THE AUTHOR

Several years ago, I thought I might write a biography of Dr. Seuss. I convened a focus group of first graders and asked what they would most like to know. Many were curious about how he made his books. One kid imagined that Dr. Seuss had a writing-and-printing-and-binding machine in his house! The great doctor would have approved, for he himself often gave fanciful answers to serious questions. He once told an interviewer that he got all his ideas in a mountain village in Switzerland called Uber Gletch, where he went every summer to have his cuckoo clock repaired. I rushed to Uber Gletch and, sure enough, a friendly Uber Gletcher presented me with a top-notch idea: I should tell the story of how Dr. Seuss created his most celebrated work, *The Cat in the Hat.* I gathered every book and article I could find. I searched for funny and unexpected details because, as Dr. Seuss pointed out, getting kids to turn the page is essential. I stuck mostly to the truth, leavened with a pinch of Seussian mischief. I tried to follow Dr. Seuss's advice to authors, "Write, rewrite, reject, re-reject, and polish incessantly." Whenever I found myself stuck, I copied the master. I put on an outrageous hat.

Judy Sierra
Portland, Oregon

A NOTE FROM
THE ILLUSTRATOR

I grew up reading Dr. Seuss books. His art and humor were very much a part of who I was as a child. The curved lines of his impossibly tilted world and the zany personalities of his characters have surely influenced my own art.

I feel so privileged to explore Ted Geisel's process as he created *The Cat in the Hat*. He had some big challenges to overcome! The list of permitted words must have been daunting for someone whose vocabulary seemed to begin where the dictionary ended! What a task to create a story so tightly woven that each word had to be exactly the right one in exactly the right place, with the right rhyme.

Giant lists and giant typewriters seem fitting for a giant undertaking. I imagine his characters dutifully following him up the stairs to his studio, where they waited to see what would become of them!

I would have loved looking over Ted's shoulder when he got his first bound copy of *The Cat in the Hat* and seeing the look on his face when he and the finished Cat came face to face for the first time.

Kevin Hawkes
Gorham, Maine

BOOKS WRITTEN AND ILLUSTRATED BY DR. SEUSS

And to Think That I Saw It on Mulberry Street

The 500 Hats of Bartholomew Cubbins

The Seven Lady Godivas

The King's Stilts

Horton Hatches the Egg

McElligot's Pool

Thidwick the Big-Hearted Moose

Bartholomew and the Oobleck

If I Ran the Zoo

Scrambled Eggs Super!

Horton Hears a Who!

On Beyond Zebra!

If I Ran the Circus

The Cat in the Hat

How the Grinch Stole Christmas!

The Cat in the Hat Comes Back

Yertle the Turtle and Other Stories

Happy Birthday to You!

One Fish Two Fish Red Fish Blue Fish

Green Eggs and Ham

The Sneetches and Other Stories

Dr. Seuss's Sleep Book

Dr. Seuss's ABC

Hop on Pop

Fox in Socks

I Had Trouble in Getting to Solla Sollew

The Cat in the Hat Songbook

The Foot Book

I Can Lick 30 Tigers Today! And Other Stories

I Can Draw It Myself

Mr. Brown Can Moo! Can You?

The Lorax

Marvin K. Mooney Will You Please Go Now!

Did I Ever Tell You How Lucky You Are?

The Shape of Me and Other Stuff

There's a Wocket in My Pocket!

Oh, the Thinks You Can Think!

The Cat's Quizzer

I Can Read with My Eyes Shut!

Oh Say Can You Say?

Hunches in Bunches

The Butter Battle Book

You're Only Old Once!

Oh, the Places You'll Go!

The Bippolo Seed and Other Lost Stories

Horton and the Kwuggerbug and More Lost Stories

What Pet Should I Get?